An Illustrated
History
of
Ireland

Designed by Philip Clucas

Edited by David Gibbon

Heraldic Artwork by Myra Maguire

Featuring the Photography of Neil Sutherland
and Michael Diggin

for Breda

4943 An Illustrated History of Ireland
This edition published in 1997 by CLB,
distributed in the USA by BHB International Inc.,
30 Edison Drive, Wayne, New Jersey 07470
Copyright © CLB Publishing, Godalming, Surrey, U.K.
A division of Quadrillion Publishing Ltd.
Printed in Hong Kong
All rights reserved
ISBN 1-85833-787-9

An Illustrated History of Ireland

John Grenham

CLB

Mullaghmore Castle on the coast of Co. Sligo, set in the
midst of mountains, sea and sky.

Contents

The Skellig Rocks, off the Kerry coast.

The Earliest Peoples and the Celts

Until about 12,000 B.C. Ireland, like the rest of northern Europe, was still in the grip of the Ice Age and was joined physically, with Britain, to the Continent. Only when the ice had retreated and the seas risen, about 8,000 B.C., did it become a separate island, separated from the British peninsula (as it then was) by the narrow North Channel. The earliest settlers, the Mesolithic people, appear to have arrived at about this period, migrating across the Channel from Scotland into northern Ireland. The island was still covered in dense woods, and the new arrivals travelled through it by water, living by fishing, and dwelt on lake and river shores and by the sea. Traces of them

Poulnabrone Dolmen, Co. Clare, the classic skeleton of a Neolithic tomb.

are found today, principally in the north, though some evidence of their way of life has been found as far south as Carlow.

The first firm knowledge of our early forebears, however, comes with the arrival of the Neolithic peoples, about 3,500 B.C. These were the first farmers, growing crops, domesticating animals, using more sophisticated

stone tools than their predecessors. It was at this period that the clearance of the thick forest covering most of the country began. Over the following 3,000 years a whole succession of colonizing invasions took place, bringing with them mature cultures and societies, evidence of which is still visible in the Irish countryside today. Thousands of megalithic tombs (literally 'built with great stones') are still to be found throughout the country, the most famous being Newgrange, over 40 feet high and covering more than an acre, oriented so that sunlight penetrates to the inner chamber only on the days of the winter and summer solstices. The social complexity and planning required to create such elaborate structures is clear, and those who built them must have had sophisticated laws, religion and societies.

The first impact of Newgrange (this page and facing page bottom) is its sheer size, but the elaborately detailed and mysterious decoration is equally impressive. Other structures, such as Drombeg stone circle in Co. Cork (facing page top), are smaller and simpler, but no less mute regarding their origins.

Without a written language, however, their history is lost to us, apart from the silent evidence of their monuments. From these we can see that they were expert miners, metalworkers, builders, and traders – a rich mixture of peoples and cultures covering more than twenty centuries.

The Celts

About the year 600 B.C. came the first of the peoples who were to determine the character of the country for the next two millennia. These were the Celts, who brought with them complex, clearly defined laws and religion, expertise in making iron and weapons, a warrior tradition and strong tribal networks. As with earlier Neolithic invaders, the newcomers did not simply replace the earlier inhabitants. Even where one culture became dominant, as did Celtic, the descendants of the earlier peoples remained, adapting and assimilating. The *Lebor Gabhála* or 'Book of Invasions', written in the ninth century A.D. but drawing on much earlier traditions, is the first account of the arrival of the Celts. Although much of it is undoubtedly mythological, nonetheless with its aid it is possible tentatively to distinguish four

separate waves of Celtic settlement in the six centuries before Christ.

The first of these peoples were known as 'Pretani', and later called *Cruithnigh* by the Irish annalists. They were firmly established in the country before 500 B.C. and appear to have made their way into eastern Ulster from Scotland. To the Romans, these were the tribes later known as Picts. In Ireland, their descendants were the Dál Riada tribes, dominating north eastern Ulster up to the ninth and tenth centuries A.D. More extensive evidence has survived about the second wave of Celtic settlement. The new peoples called themselves *Euerni*, a name written later by the annalists as *Érainn*. Their new home they called after themselves, *Eueriio*. For the Greek and Roman cartographers, this became *Ierin* and *Iouernia*, and from this latter was eventually derived the Latin name for the country, Hibernia. The modern Irish name for the island evolved more directly, from the Celtic *Eueriio* through the Old Irish *Ériu* to *Éire*; from *Éire* came 'Ireland', through the simple addition of the English suffix '-land'.

The earliest map of Ireland, drawn in the second century A.D. by Claudius Ptolemy of Alexandria, shows branches of the *Érainn* widely spread throughout the country, but it is with the south that they appear to have had the strongest connection. Ptolemy locates the *Iverni*, treated as a single tribe, in the present county of Cork, and subsequent research has identified several sub-tribes in the area. From these tribes have come some of the oldest place names in the country – the *Ciarraige* giving their name to modern Kerry, the *Fir Máige* to the town and barony of Fermoy in Co. Cork, the *Uí Bairche* (or *Brigantes* in Ptolemy's map) to the barony of Bargy in south Wexford.

From the strength of the associations of the *Érainn* with the south of the country, it is reasonable to suppose that it was in the south that they first established themselves, probably in the fifth century B.C., afterwards extending their conquest to the rest of the island. This view is reinforced by evidence which suggests that the

Ogham stones (above right) record the earliest memorial inscriptions in Ireland. Prehistoric forts such as Dun Aengus on the Aran Islands (bottom right and far right) suggest, through their size and isolation, the scale of the violence they were built to withstand.

Érainn were in fact part of the *Belgae*, the name applied by the Romans to large sections of the Continental Celts. *Bolg*, one of the most common of the Celtic names for their sun-god, was given in the later genealogical tracts as one of the mythical ancestors of these people; the derivation of the name from *Bolgi* (Celtic) to *Belgae* (Latin) and *Fir Bolg* (Irish) is suggestive, at the very least.

The third Celtic wave of colonization took place, it is believed, around the year 300 B.C. These were the *Laighin*, whose name comes from the *laigne*, or spears, with which they armed themselves. From their association from the earliest times with what is now the modern province of Leinster (in Irish *Laighin*), it may be taken that this was the area in which they first landed, coming directly, it is thought, from the western part of Normandy. They extended their power across the island gradually, moving towards the western seaboard, and in the process forcing the *Érainn* or *Fir Bolg* into the remoter parts of the country. Tradition from this period ascribes to the *Érainn* the building of the great stone forts still to be found in many of the most isolated parts of Ireland.

Within a few centuries, Laiginian tribes were well established in many parts of the country, and their names have survived to the present in both placenames and surnames. The modern diocese of Ossory, covering almost all of County Kilkenny, takes its name from the *Osraige*, one of the most prominent of these tribes, while the barony of Idrone in Co. Carlow is the old homeland of the *Uí Drona*. From the *Uí Ceinnselaigh*, a tribe inhabiting parts of south Wexford, comes the modern surname Kinsella, still common in the Wexford area. The spread of the Laiginian peoples is also reflected in the placenames of Mayo, Roscommon and Galway, but it is in south Leinster that their power held out to the tenth century.

The Gaeil

The last of the major Celtic settlements in Ireland took place about the year 50 B.C., and was a direct result of Roman attempts to dominate the Celtic tribes of Gaul. Among the many peoples uprooted and dispersed by this attempt were a group who appear to have been known to themselves as the *Feni*, who came directly from the Continent to Ireland, arriving, according to popular tradition, in south Kerry and the Boyne estuary.

The earlier inhabitants of the country, who resisted fiercely the incursions of the newcomers, called these people the *Gaodhail* or *Gael*, from the language they spoke, Gaedelg, in English 'Gaelic'. Although details of the history of the first centuries A.D. remain obscure, it is clear that the influence and power of the *Gaeil* spread steadily over the next three centuries at the expense of the *Laighin* and the *Érainn*, expanding northwards from Kerry into Tipperary and Limerick, and westwards into Roscommon and Galway, until by the fifth century they were dominant throughout most of Ireland and had established the dynasties and tribal groupings which determined the politics and culture of the country until the arrival of the Normans.

As they pushed their way west and north through Ireland, the *Gaeil* also made their presence felt on the western coasts of Britain, where the decline of Roman power left many relatively wealthy areas vulnerable to attack. Sporadic raids carried out during the third century developed into permanent settlements in the fourth and fifth, with the largest and most powerful colonies in southwestern Wales and western Scotland, although Cornwall, Devon, Hampshire and the islands of Man, Orkney and Shetland also show signs of this expansion. The main evidence for it today is the distribution of Ogham stones. These are memorial stones, with the name of the person commemorated inscribed by representing Latin letters with groups of lines set at different angles. Virtually all of the stones found in the British Isles are of Irish origin, and their distribution closely reflects the limits of Gaelic power in Britain.

The most important and enduring distinction within the *Gaeil* was between the southern tribes and those of the north and west. In the south they gave themselves the name *Eoghanacht*, or 'people of Eogan', in honour of their ancestor-deity Eogan (in English 'Owen'), and, about the year 400 A.D founded at Cashel the dynasty which held power through most of the southern part of the country from the fifth to the twelfth centuries. In later historical times, the powerful Munster families of O'Sullivan, McCarthy and O'Connell can claim descent from the *Eoghanacht*.

Similarly, in the midlands, west and north, the tribes of the *Gaeil* were known as *Connachta*, or 'people of Conn', in myth the brother of Eogan. Their name endures in the modern province of Connacht. By far the most important of the *Connachta* tribes were the *Uí Néill*,

The notches along the edges of Ogham stones represent letters of the Roman alphabet. Apart from Ireland, they are found only along the west coast of Britain, in areas of Irish colonization.

('O'Neill') claiming descent from Niall Noigiallach ('Niall of the Nine Hostages'), who appears to have lived in the early fifth century, and is given in the genealogical tracts as a son of Eochu Mugmedon ('lord of slaves'), himself several generations descended from Conn. Among Niall's brothers were Ailill, Brion, and Fiachra, founders of the important *Connachta* tribes of *Uí Ailella*, *Uí Briain*, and *Uí Fiachrach*.

The rise of the *Uí Néill* took place through the fifth and sixth centuries, with the conquest of a line of kingdoms stretching from Sligo Bay on the west coast, north to Inishowen in Donegal, and eastwards as far as the Irish Sea. Separate dynasties emerged in the northern and eastern kingdoms, to be known by the later annalists as the northern and southern *Uí Néill*, the former with

their seat at Aileach in Inishowen, the latter based at Tara in County Meath. From the beginning of the seventh century, the *Uí Néill* claimed the high-kingship of all Ireland, alternating between the northern and southern branches. The claim was never accepted by all the other local dynasties, in particular by the *Eoghanacht*, dominant in the southern part of the island, but no serious challenge to the power of the *Uí Néill* emerged until the tenth century.

Although the *Eoghanacht* and the *Uí Néill* were the two predominant tribal groupings, a number of others were locally powerful, particularly in the northeast of the country, where the *Oirialla* controlled territory now included in counties Tyrone, Armagh, Fermanagh and Monaghan, and the *Ulaidh* inhabited what is now counties Down and Antrim. These peoples almost certainly originally possessed lands further to the west, but were displaced by the aggressive expansion to the north and east of the *Uí Néill*.

Gaelic Society

Within these large areas many smaller divisions existed, known as *tuatha*, of which there were about 150 throughout the country; the names of many of these are reflected today in the names of the baronies which make up the modern counties. Each of these *tuatha* had its own ruler or petty king, who owed allegiance to a more powerful leader, an over-king of three or more *tuatha*, who in turn was subordinate to the king of the province, generally of the *Eoghanacht* or the *Uí Néill*. Such an arrangement was clearly ripe for potential conflict, and continuous warfare between *tuatha*, over-kings and provinces was endemic in Ireland until the end of the Middle Ages.

The tribal culture of the *Gaeil*, like that of all Celts, was highly developed and complex, and dominated life throughout the country for fifteen centuries, until its final collapse in the seventeenth century. In essence, it consisted of a highly codified legal system which regulated relationships within and between classes, families, larger kin-groups, and *tuatha*. Three classes existed: the professionals (*aos dána*), made up of poets, historians, jurists, musicians and, before the arrival of Christianity, druids; the free (*saor aicme*), warriors, owning land and cattle; and the unfree (*daor aicme*), slaves, many of whom were prisoners or the descendants of prisoners taken in war.

Above: Staigue Fort, Co. Kerry and the Grianan of Aileach, Co. Donegal (facing page). The Grianan became the chief seat of the northern *Uí Néill*, whose territory took in counties Derry, Donegal, Tyrone and Armagh.

The professionals were widely honoured and, with the exception of the jurists, travelled freely between the various tribes; it was not until the beginning of the eighteenth century that itinerant poets and musicians finally lost their position and privilege. Amongst the free, rights and responsibilities pivoted on the *fine*, or kin-group. For most purposes, this consisted of men who had a great-grandfather in common, that is, up to and including second cousins. Each member of this group bore responsibility for the actions, debts and contracts of the other members, and loyalty to the group was the primary social obligation. The immediate family, as we would understand it, was secondary to the *fine*. Thus, kingship of the *tuath* or the province passed from one member of the *fine* to another, rather than necessarily to the eldest male heir. The vivid sense of kinship and mutual obligation engendered by such a system are clearly visible throughout Irish history, and even in Irish society today.

Portrait of St John from the Book of Kells. The hairstyle and
dress are a close reflection of contemporary Irish custom.

Christianity, Placenames and Surnames

 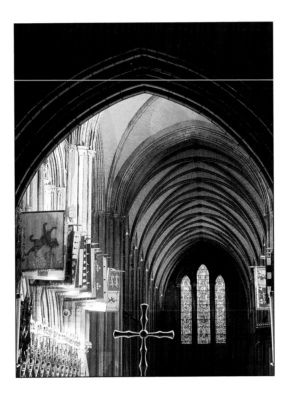 

Of all the outside influences on Gaelic culture up to the time of the Tudor conquest, the most powerful was the introduction of Christianity. It was Laoighire, son of Niall Noigiallach and first *Uí Néill* ruler of Tara who reputedly received the Christian missionary Patrick in the year 432; in any case, early missionary activity, largely emanating from Britain, seems to have been concentrated in the northern part of the country, in what was later to be the territory of the *Oirialla*, the *Ulaidh* and the southern *Uí Néill*. Because the earlier pagan religion was tolerant and accommodating, like many polytheistic systems reckoning one god more or

St Patrick's Cathedral, Dublin, dating from 1191, with the banners of the knights of the Order of St Patrick hanging above the choir stalls.

less to be of little importance, Christianity made rapid headway. By the end of the sixth century it was solidly established throughout the country.

In the long term the introduction of Christianity posed problems for Gaelic society; there was simply no place in the existing scheme of things for monastic communities separated from their kin, following a way of life so different from that which surrounded them. In

The monks on the bare Atlantic
rock of Skellig Michael (left)
lived a life of breathtaking
austerity and isolation on the
very edge of the known world.
The High Cross of Kilfenora
(above and top) shows how the
Vikings influenced the art of the
Irish Church, their principal
victim.

the end, the solution proved to be that of giving to the most powerful churchmen, bishops and abbots, a status equivalent to that of the king of a *tuath*, with a proportionate status to lower members of the church hierarchy. In turn, the church adapted itself to the existing social structure, and many bishoprics and abbotships remained within the same extended kin-group. As a result, the church in Ireland acquired a large measure of temporal power from an early date.

Above: the ruins of Mellifont Abbey, Co. Louth – the first Cistercian abbey to have been founded in Ireland.

Monastic ideals very quickly took root as the church grew, with over 800 monasteries founded by the end of the sixth century; abbots soon wielded considerably more power than bishops, as confederations emerged in which a single large monastery might have control of 30 or more smaller establishments. It was this system which provided the closest equivalent in early Ireland to large-scale settlement. Gaelic culture was rural and agricultural, based around the *fine*, and gave rise to no towns. The large monasteries, such as Armagh, Clonmacnoise and Bangor, provided commercial and administrative networks, and were themselves centres of trade, law, and, above all, learning.

It was for this learning, and for their piety, that Irish monks very quickly acquired an international reputation. The copying of manuscript was an important part of the functions of the monasteries, and the sixth and seventh

centuries produced such masterpieces of illuminated manuscript as the *Book of Kells* and the *Book of Durrow*, vivid evidence of the monks' extraordinary veneration of learning, and of the rich fusion of Christianity with Celtic tradition.

The security and prosperity of the monasteries at home was the driving force behind the great expansion of Irish influence in Britain and continental Europe between the sixth and tenth centuries. Exile was the ultimate sacrifice for the monks, and it was the quest for such a sacrifice, not missionary fervour, that led so many of them abroad in these years. Once established, however, their fervour and dedication achieved great missionary success, with the conversion of the Picts, and the creation of enduring monastic foundations throughout areas now part of Italy, Austria, Germany, France, Holland, Belgium and Spain, as well as Britain. Even as their fame as religious pioneers and scholars grew, the Irish monks retained many of the distinctive features of their own institutions, for example in refusing to accept the authority of the Pope in calculating the date of Easter. Irish obstinacy was well known; Pope Honorius I wrote to the Irish in 634 'earnestly exhorting them not to think their small number, placed in the utmost borders of the earth, wiser than all the ancient and modern churches of Christ, throughout the world.'

Placenames

The rapid growth of the church is also the source of many of the commonest placenames in Ireland today. For example, two of the most familiar prefixes: 'Kill-', and 'Donagh-', come from Irish words for 'church': *cill* and *domhnach*, the latter meaning literally 'Sunday', and used by extension for the place of worship on that day. Placenames with elements such as these almost invariably originated between the fifth and ninth centuries. Many of the names in everyday use today, in particular those for the smallest geographical unit, the townland, however, are of much greater age, in all probability as old as human habitation itself. This is truest of those names which are derived from natural features, containing such elements as *druim* (Drum-), a height; *cnoc* (Knock-), a hill; *tulach* (Tulla-), a mound; *gleann* (Glen-), a glen. The age of some of these can be gauged from the fact that some of the features they describe no longer exist. Thus 'Derry', in Irish *doire*, meaning 'oakwood', is common and widespread

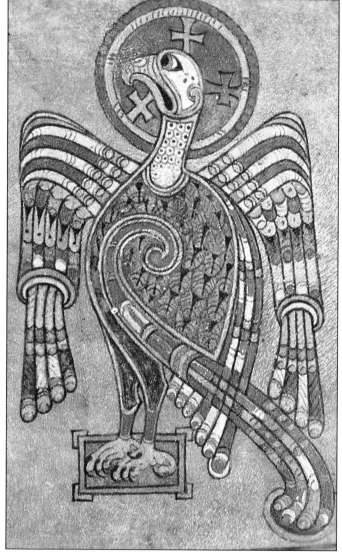

Facing page bottom: the symbol of the evangelist St Matthew, from the Book of Kells. The heavy walls and strategic situation of many Church settlements, such as those at Kells (facing page top) and on the Rock of Cashel (above), reflect the Church's secular power; Cashel, before becoming the ecclesiastical capital of Munster, had been the seat of the dominant Eoghanacht dynasty for almost six centuries.

throughout the country, even though the forests described in the names have long since vanished.

Of later date, and more fluid, are those names recording human activity: *gort* (Gort-), a field; *baile* (Bally-), place or farm; *ráth* (Rath-), a fort; *lios* (Lis-), an enclosure. In some cases history is itself inscribed in the name: *tamhlacht*, (Tallagh/Tamlaght), means 'famine grave', evidence that famine was familiar in the country from the earliest times. Such names as these proliferated as the population increased, changing and adapting to the different uses made of the land. It was not until the seventeenth century that the demands of the English administrative and legal systems began to enforce standardization of these names, a process in which many thousands of the old names were lost.

Surnames

Although up to the tenth century surnames in Ireland were not hereditary, the influence of the church, dating from this period, can still be seen in many common modern Irish surnames, in particular those beginning with 'Gil-' or 'Kil-', an anglicised version of the Irish Gi*olla*, meaning follower or devotee. Thus Gilmartin, in Irish *Mac Giolla Mhártain*, means 'son of a follower of (St) Martin'. Similarly, the church is the origin of all of those names starting with 'Mul-', a version of the Irish

Maol, meaning bald, and applied to the monks because of their distinctive tonsure. Thus Mulrennan (*Ó Maoilbhréanainn*) means 'descendant of a follower of St Brendan'.

While many of the names appearing in accounts of this time appear similar in form to modern Irish names, incorporating in particular the prefix 'mac' (meaning 'son of'), in fact they were not hereditary, lasting only

one generation. Thus Turlough mac Airt, was Turlough, son of Art; his own son would be Conor mac Turlough, Conor son of Turlough.

Nonetheless, Ireland was one of the first European countries in which a system of fixed hereditary surnames developed. The earliest names appear to be those incorporating 'Ó' or its earlier form *Ua*, meaning 'grandson'. The first recorded fixed surname is O'Clery (*Ó Cléirigh*), as noted by the Annals, which record the death of Tigherneach Ua Cléirigh, Lord of Aidhne in Co. Galway in the year 916. It seems likely that this is the oldest surname recorded anywhere in Europe.

By the eleventh century many families had acquired true surnames as we would know them today. All of these surnames incorporate the same two basic elements, 'O' or 'Mac', together with the personal name

of the ancestor from whom descent is indicated. In many cases this ancestor can be quite accurately identified, and the origin of the name dated precisely. Thus, at the start of the eleventh century, Brian Boru possessed no surname, being simply 'Brian, High-King of the Irish', his grandson Teigue called himself *Ua Briain* in memory of his illustrious grandfather, and the name became hereditary thereafter. Similarly, the

The profusion of Irish surnames originating in the Church is a clear reflection of the depth of its early influence. The ruins of simple monastic settlements such as that at Kilree, Co. Kilkenny (left) are common and widespread. Even St Patrick's Cathedral in Dublin (facing page), now the national symbol of the Church of Ireland, stands on the site of a much simpler pre-Norman establishment.

O'Neills derive their surname from Niall Glún Dubh, who died in 919.

Due to linguistic changes, the origins of many of the personal names such as Niall or Brian which form the stem of the surname remain obscure, but two broad categories can be distinguished: descriptive and occupational. In the first category, we can guess that the progenitor of the Traceys (*Ó Treasaigh*) was a formidable character, *treasach* meaning 'warlike', while the ancestor of the Duffs must have been dark-featured, since *dubh*, the root of the name, means black or dark. Among the occupations recorded in names are the churchmen dealt with above, clerks (Clery, *Ó Cléirigh*, from *cléireach*), bards (Ward, *Mac an Bháird*, from *bard*), spokesman (MacCloran, *Mac Labhráin*, from the Irish *labhraidh*), and smiths (McGowan, *Mac*

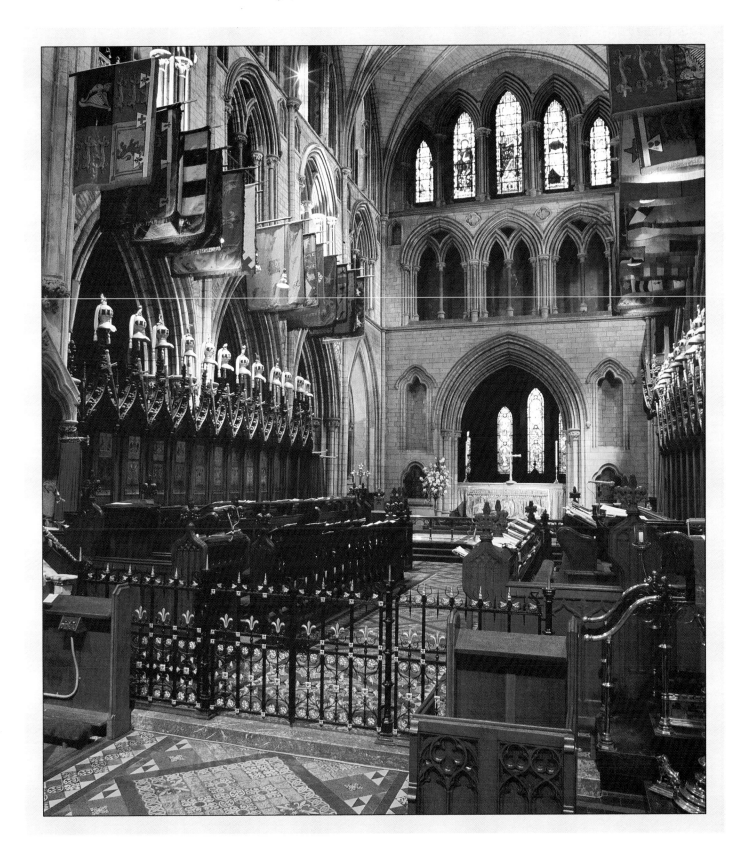

Gabhann, from *gabha*). One category of name, common in English, which is extremely rare among Irish names is the toponymic, deriving from the name of a locality. It seems likely that this reflects the fact that, for the Gaeil, who you were related to was much more important than where you came from.

Although the immediate reason for the early adoption of hereditary names in Ireland may have been a rapidly expanding population, it can also be seen as the logical outcome of a process at work from the times of the earliest tribal names. Originally, these indicated identification with a common god, often connected with an animal valued by the tribe, as in the case of the *Osrái*, or 'deer-people', for example. Next came identification with a divine ancestor, the *Bóinnrí*, for instance, claiming descent from the goddess Bóinn, the divinised river Boyne. Later the ancestor was merely legendary, as for the *Eoghanacht*, while later still the tribe claimed direct descent from a historical ancestor, as in the case of the *Uí Néill*. This slow emergence of kin-relationships out of religion and myth into the realm of history would seem to reach its logical conclusion with the adoption of hereditary surnames, permanent proof of verifiable ties of blood. On a more mundane level, of course, such proof was a valuable political asset, since it demonstrated membership of a powerful kin-group. Even today, the fact that all Gaelic names, with few exceptions, begin with O or Mac is undeniable and continuing proof of the significance of family and kin for the Irish.

Although it began early, the process of the creation of surnames was slow, and continued for over six hundred years. As the population grew and new families were formed, they sought to consolidate their identity by adopting hereditary surnames of their own, usually by simply adding *Mac* to the first name of the founding ancestor. In the course of this process, then, many surnames were created which are in fact offshoots of more common names. Thus, for example, the MacMahons and the McConsidines are descended from the O'Brien family, the former from Mahon O'Brien, who died in 1129, the latter from Constantine O'Brien, who died in 1193. The continuing division and sub-division of the most powerful Gaelic families like this is almost certainly the reason for the great proliferation of Gaelic surnames.

Physical features such as the Co. Waterford waterfall (top) and the Comeragh Mountains (right) are obvious and frequent sources of placenames, but ownership was often the most vivid distinguishing characteristic, as for MacGillycuddy's Reeks (above).

The massive defensive power of Blarney Castle, Co. Cork,
built by Cormac MacCarthy in 1446, was no luxury.

Invasion, Plantation and War

For at least 1,400 years, up to the ninth century, the civilization of Ireland remained uniformly Celtic. Then, in the year 795, came the first of the Viking attacks, on Lambay Island in Dublin Bay. This was the beginning of more than two centuries of attack and invasion which had a devastating effect on Ireland, and on the Irish monasteries in particular.

'Viking' (from the Old Norse *víkingr*) means 'sea-rover' or 'pirate', and this is precisely what these people were. Ethnically they were Teutons, Danish, Swedish and Norwegian farmers, fishermen and sea-merchants, who were forced onto the open sea in search of a

Round Castle, near the entrance to Bannow Harbour, Co. Kerry, part of the defences of the Earls of Desmond, who created what was in effect a separate state in south Munster.

livelihood by over-population and shortage of arable land. From the eighth century, their plundering raids terrorized much of the known world, reaching as far as America, North Africa, and Constantinople.

In Ireland, the annalists distinguished two groups among the raiding Vikings, the *Lochlannaigh*, or Norwegians, and the *Danair*, or Danes, the Norwegians

being described as fair, the Danish as dark. Initially the Norwegians dominated, and their raids were sporadic and unsystematic. From about 830, however, a new phase of large-scale attacks, involving the use of fleets of longships, began, and the Vikings penetrated deep inland through the use of rivers and lakes. Attracted by the wealth of the monasteries and churches, they plundered them steadily. From this period date the first of the Vikings' fortified settlements. In 852, the Danes wrested control of one of these settlements, the military and trading post of Dublin, from the Norwegians, under their king Olaf (in Irish *Amhlaoibh*), and founded the Danish kingdom of Dublin which was to last three hundred years, until the coming of the Anglo-Normans.

For the next 100 years, up to the middle of the tenth century, the Vikings consolidated and extended their power through unremitting aggression. From about 950 on, however, the east Clare Gaelic sept of the *Dál gCais* began its rise to power, capturing first the Kingship of Munster from the *Eoghanacht* and then, with Brian Boru, taking the high-kingship of Ireland from the *Uí Néill* in 1002. Brian fused the disparate Gaelic forces into a single confederate army, and defeated the combined might of the Norwegian and Danish forces in the battle of Clontarf on April 23, 1014, breaking the power of the Vikings permanently.

Although their political power declined rapidly after this, as a people the Vikings were soon thoroughly absorbed into the religious and political life of the country, adopting the Irish language and Irish customs, intermarrying and intermingling. Many modern Irish surnames reflect this, with McLoughlin (*Mac Lochlainn*) and McIvor (*Mac Íomhair*), for instance, deriving from a combination of the Gaelic patronymic with a Norse personal name. To them also we owe all of the earliest towns in the country: Dublin, Wexford, Waterford, Cork and Limerick all began as Viking settlements, and even after their absorption into the Gaelic culture the commercial interests of the newcomers kept them centred in these areas.

Ireland Before the Normans

For a century and a half after the battle of Clontarf the Irish provincial kings were locked in internecine warfare which proved just as devastating as the attacks of the Viking raiders. The man deposed by Brian Boru, Malachy II, resumed the high-kingship after Brian's death at Clontarf, but he was to be the last undisputed occupant of the throne. After this there were always at least two claimants at war with each other.

By now the large-scale divisions of the country had evolved considerably, although the earlier tribal territories were still the basis of political geography. There were five major areas: Leinster, Meath, Munster, Ulster and Connacht. Leinster, covering most of the traditional territory of the *Laighin*, was ruled by the MacMurrough family, based at Ferns in Co. Wexford. Meath was still the preserve of the southern *Uí Néill*, of whom Malachy II was the last to aspire to the high kingship. In Connacht, the ruling family was the O'Connors, although a number of powerful sub-kingdoms existed, in which their authority remained weak. One such sub-kingdom was *Breifne*, covering parts of the modern counties of Sligo, Leitrim, Cavan and Monaghan, and ruled by the O'Rourkes. Munster was chiefly under the power of the O'Brien family, the dynasty founded by Brian Boru, but their supremacy was continually challenged by the powerful *Eoghanacht* family of the MacCarthys. In Ulster, four individual kingdoms existed, Tirconnell, Tirowen, Uriel and Ulaidh, ruled, respectively, by the O'Donnells (part of the northern *Uí Néill*), the MacLochlainns, the O'Carrolls, and the MacDonlevys.

The Normans

The Normans were descendants of Vikings who, by the early tenth century, had established themselves firmly in a large area around the lower Seine in France, later known as Normandy, and, like the Vikings in Ireland, had been assimilated into French society. They soon acquired a reputation for military sophistication, and were active in many of the European wars. In 1066, with only 5,000 men, William, Duke of Normandy, took the crown of England, and over the next century the Normans set up a strong kingdom in England, and solidly established themselves in Scotland and Wales.

It was the incessant warfare among the provincial kings, and the resulting shifts in power and allegiance, which ultimately led to the arrival of the Normans in

Round towers (facing page) were a desperate defensive response by the Irish monasteries to the growing threat of Viking invaders. Their effectiveness in providing refuge during raids seems doubtful.

Above: the marriage of Aoife, daughter of Dermot
MacMurrough, to Strongbow, depicted by Daniel Maclise
as the symbolic source of Ireland's subsequent
catastrophes. Right: the Norman castle at Trim, built in
the thirteenth century by the de Lacys, is one of the
largest in Ireland.

Ireland. In 1166 Mac Lochlainn, king of Tirowen and
claimant of the high-kingship, was killed in a rebellion of
the northern sub-kings and the O'Connors of Connacht.
As a result, his ally Dermot MacMurrough, king of
Leinster, was expelled from his kingdom, and went to
seek help across the Irish sea. When he had outlined to
Henry II and his barons the profits to be made from
involvement in Ireland, they lost little time in organizing
a succession of expeditions. The first of these, under
Robert Fitzstephen, landed at Bannow Bay in Wexford
on May 1, 1169. It was quickly followed by others, and
with the help of MacMurrough's men the Normans took
Wexford town and launched successful attacks north
and east into Offaly and Ossory. The Irish, under the

new high-king Rory O'Connor, put up stiff resistance, however, and it was not until the arrival of Strongbow, Richard Fitzgilbert de Clare, in August 1170, that the Norman invasion was assured of success. By the autumn of 1171 Strongbow was master of Dublin, Wexford and Waterford, and was launching attacks into *Breifne* and Meath.

In October 1171 Henry II himself arrived to secure his own power, over both the Norman invaders and the Irish kings, and quickly achieved both objectives. Many

their methods of government to suit Irish conditions – accepting, for example, the provincial divisions – in those areas where they had greatest control they soon began to superimpose the political divisions which had existed in England since the Anglo-Saxons: the shires. By the early fourteenth century there were twelve of these: Dublin, Carlow, Louth, Roscommon, Cork, Kerry, Tipperary, Limerick, Kildare, Waterford, Meath and Connacht, all but the last in more or less the form they are known today.

Above: the seal and (right) the tomb of Strongbow, displaying the Normans' pride in their military prowess.

of the Irish, including O'Brien, MacCarthy and O'Rourke, submitted to him, and Strongbow's power was curbed by confining him to Leinster, with Dublin, Wexford and Waterford removed from his jurisdiction.

From now on, the process for the Normans was one of consolidation and expansion. Castle-building was one of the fundamental elements of their practice; as they took control of an area, a fortress, initially in wood, later in stone, was erected to help retain that control. Around the castles, churches and other buildings were built, and from these grew many of the present towns of Ireland, for example Athlone, Carrickfergus, and Nenagh. It was the Normans, too, who began the creation of what are now the counties of Ireland. Although they adapted

Over the next 300 years, the history of Ireland is a kaleidoscope of Gaelic and Norman advance and retreat. Until the thirteenth century Norman progress was steady, encroaching on the old Gaelic families, displacing and subduing them. From the second half of the thirteenth century, however, the native lords began a resistance struggle which had Leinster, Connacht and Meath in virtual continual revolt, and which culminated in the invasion of Edward Bruce, invited from Scotland in 1314 by the Gaelic lords. The invasion failed, but demonstrated graphically the tenuousness of Norman control over many areas of the country.

Theoretically, Ireland was governed by English law, and subject to a royal administration centred in Dublin.

In fact, effective royal jurisdiction was confined to the Pale, an area centred around Dublin which grew and shrank with the fortunes of the English in Ireland; by 1537, with the resurgence of native influence, the Pale included only Dublin and some parts of counties Meath, Louth and Kildare.

Outside the Pale, many of the Norman lords governed their lands independently of English law; the Fitzgeralds, Earls of Desmond, rulers of most of counties Kerry, Limerick, Cork and Waterford, operated what was in effect an independent state in the southern part of the country through most of the fifteenth and sixteenth centuries. Apart from the great Norman lords – Burke and Bermingham in Connacht, Fitzgerald, Fitzmaurice and Barry in Munster, the Butlers in Kilkenny – many of the original Gaelic families retained and extended effective control over their traditional lands, while others,

Above and above left: Blarney Castle. The MacCarthys retained possession of their lands into the seventeenth century, due in part to such Norman-style defences.

displaced by the Normans, moved to neighbouring areas and drove out the original inhabitants. It was in Ulster that the Normans made least headway; the O'Neills and O'Donnells in particular had successfully resisted their expansion, and continually pushed back the borders of the Norman lands.

Ultimately more successful than military pressure was the attraction exerted by Gaelic society. Slowly over the centuries, the Norman families outside the Pale intermarried with the Irish and adopted their language and customs, until by the sixteenth century they had more in common with the native Irish than with England, in whose name they held power.

The extent of the intermingling of Norman and
Gaelic is illustrated graphically in the history of surnames
of Norman origin. These are numerous and widespread
throughout the country, and most of them were created
in the aftermath of the Norman invasion; names such as
Browne, Burke, Cusack, Keating, Power, Walsh.
Whatever their current form, virtually all of these
originated in Norman-French, either linked to a particular
placename in Normandy or Wales, or as a French
descriptive. Thus *de Burgo* or *de Burgh*, the original
version of Burke, comes from Tonburg in Normandy,
while *le Poer*, the original for Power, comes from *le
povre*, meaning 'the poor one'. The names now most
obviously of Norman origin are those beginning with
'Fitz', a corruption of the French *fils*, meaning 'son', and
used by the Normans in the same way as the Gaels used
Mac. Of course, as well as those of purely Norman
origin, the twelfth-century invaders also included
many of Breton and Flemish extraction. Irish names of
Breton origin include Dillon (*de Leon*, from Leon in
Brittany) and Brett (*le Breton*), while Flemish examples
include Fleming, Roche (*de la Roche*) and Wall (*de
Vale*).

As the Normans were assimilated into Gaelic culture
their surnames underwent the same process of
subdivision already seen in Gaelic surnames. Thus, for
example, in the thirteenth century the descendants of
Piers de Birmingham were calling themselves *Mac
Fheorais*, Irish for 'son of Piers', which was later anglicised
as 'Corish'. In the same way, Jocelyn (in Irish *Goisdelbh*)
de Angulo was the ancestor of the family of
MacGoisdealbhaigh, anglicised Costello, while the
fragmentation of the powerful *de Burgo* (Burke) family
of Connacht led to such surname offshoots as
MacWalter, MacSheoinín (later anglicised as 'Jennings'),
MacMyler and MacDavid.

**THE TERRITORIES OF THE GREAT FAMILIES OF IRELAND
IN THE FOURTEENTH CENTURY**

O'Doherty

MacSweeney

MacDonnell

MacSweeney

O'Cahan

O'DONNELL

O'NEILL

Maguire

O'Neill
Clanaboy

Earldom
of
Ulster

Barrett

Burke

O'Dowd

O'Rourke

O'Connor

O'Hara

O'Gara

MacDonagh

MacMahon

McGuinness

O'Malley

MacDermot

O'Farrell

O'Reilly

Plunket

O'Flaherty

Costello

O'Connor
Don

Preston

O'Kelly

Bermingham

Barnewall

Blake

O'Madden

Burke

St. Laurence

O'Carroll

O'Connor

Earldom
of
Kildare

O'Molloy

O'Dunn

O'Toole

O'Brien

MacNamara

O'More

Fitzgerald

O'Byrne

O'Kennedy

Fitzmaurice

Fitzgerald

Burke

Butler
of
Ormond

MacMurrogh

Earldom
of
Desmond

Roche

MacCarthy Mor

Power

O'Sullivan

Fitzgerald

O'Sullivan

Barry

MacCarthy

O'Driscoll

Tudor Plantations

Throughout the fifteenth and early sixteenth centuries, the rulers of England were too preoccupied elsewhere to devote energy and resources to Ireland, and the absorption of the Norman newcomers reflected the weakness of English power. With the accession of Henry VIII, this changed. Henry set out to turn the fiction of English rule into fact, by demanding recognition of his authority from the semi-independent Gaelic and Norman lords in return for his granting them legal title to their lands. Under this arrangement, forty of the most powerful lords accepted his authority, some of them receiving English titles also: O'Brien became Earl of Thomond, O'Neill Earl of Tyrone, Burke of Galway Earl of Clanrickard. As well as ruling indirectly through them, Henry also extended direct royal rule throughout Leinster and into parts of Munster. In the areas controlled directly by the crown strenuous efforts were made to introduce the Reformation, dissolving the monasteries and attempting to introduce doctrinal reforms. In this, neither he nor following English rulers had much success, either with the Gaelic population or with the Old English, as the descendants of the Normans were now known. From this period, the conflicts between English and Irish were sharpened by differences of religion.

Henry's daughter, Mary, began the process of plantation which was to change the social composition of the country permanently. Under this process, land held by the native or Old English lords was declared forfeit to the crown, for a variety of possible reasons, the most usual being disloyalty or rebellion. The land was then granted to English settlers, who were expected to anglicise the area. The first plantations were carried out in 1556, in counties Laois and Offaly, renamed Queen's and King's counties, and were fiercely resisted, as a result achieving only partial success. Plantation policy was continued under Elizabeth, with the largest covering the forfeited lands of the Earls of Desmond in Munster in 1586.

All of these plantations were severely disrupted by the great rebellion which broke out in 1594. Up to this period, Ulster had been least affected by the steady encroachments of the English on the native lands, and the Gaelic Ulster lords had maintained almost total independence over the centuries. Now, however, they recognized the danger to their own power, and by 1595 Hugh O'Neill, Hugh O'Donnell and Hugh Maguire were waging open war against the English. In response, Elizabeth committed massive numbers of troops, and her best generals, and the Irish were finally defeated at the battle of Kinsale in 1601. This defeat marked the end of the Gaelic lordship, and the start of the final collapse of Gaelic society.

The Ulster Plantation

In Ulster, the defeat of the Gaelic aristocracy and the subsequent escape to the continent of almost 100 of the most important leaders, left a vacuum, which Elizabeth's successor, James I, was quick to fill. In 1609 the Plantation of Ulster was declared, affecting the entire counties of Armagh, Tyrone, Fermanagh, Donegal, Cavan and Coleraine (now Derry or Londonderry). Of the estimated 3,800,000 acres involved, 1,500,000, partly or wholly infertile, were set aside for the native Irish. Over one-and-a-half million acres of the remainder was given in grants to schools, the Church of Ireland, the military, and institutions; for instance, in exchange for financial backing the entire county of Coleraine was granted to the guilds of the city of London, and renamed Londonderry. The rest of the land was set aside for colonization, with large estates granted at nominal rents on condition that the landlord let the land only to English or Scots tenants.

Unlike the earlier plantations further south, the plantation of Ulster was highly successful. Although it did not fully achieve its aim of clearing certain areas completely of the native Irish – despite the terms of the land grants many of them managed to remain as tenants – it nonetheless attracted a massive influx of settlers. A very large proportion of these were Scots Calvinists, drawn by the relative freedom from religious intolerance in what was seen very much as frontier territory, and their names, Ross, Kerr, Graham, Morrison, Stewart, still predominate throughout many areas of Ulster today.

The situation in the two northeastern counties of Ulster, Antrim and Down, was different. Connections of trade and blood had existed between Scotland and the coastal areas of these counties for centuries, and the highly successful private plantations undertaken in the counties by Sir Arthur Chichester, Hugh Montgomery, and James Hamilton from 1605 simply accelerated a process already under way.

Above: Oliver Cromwell, the Lord Protector. His name is still reviled in Ireland, both for the ruthless slaughter he inflicted and for the massive dispossessions that followed his victory. The policies of Elizabeth I (facing page) were less genocidal, but played an equally large part in bringing about the final collapse of the old order.

Apart from Ulster, the early seventeenth century also saw plantations carried out in Leitrim, Longford, King's County, Queen's County, Westmeath and Longford. These were much less thorough than those in the north, however, retaining native tenants and placenames, and achieved only limited success. In general, the settlers in these areas were English, known as the New English to distinguish them from the Catholic descendants of the Normans, the Old English.

The Wars of the Seventeenth Century

The dispossessions of Gaelic and Old English families by the plantations, and the introduction of a new colonial population into Ulster, produced enormous discontent; by the 1640s the country was ripe for rebellion. In October 1641 a rising of the native Irish began, led from the north by Sir Felim O'Neill, Rory O'More and Lord Maguire. In the fierce and bloody fighting which followed, the rebels took control of almost the whole province of Ulster, along with parts of Leinster. After a delay of two months the rebels were joined by the Old English and, by February 1642, the entire country, with the exception of parts of Cork, Donegal and Antrim, was in rebel hands. At this point the English Parliament passed the 'Adventurers' Act', promising the repayment in Irish land of money advanced by individuals to help suppress the Irish rebellion. This was the start of a process of land transfer and colonization much more extensive than anything attempted up to now.

Throughout the 1640s the Confederation of Old English and Irish, though divided among themselves, fought a bitter war, first against the crown, then against the winning side in the English Civil War, the parliamentary forces. By the time Cromwell arrived in Ireland in 1649 the Confederate forces were weak, and the efficient ferocity of Cromwell's campaign, with massacres at Drogheda, Wexford and elsewhere, broke the rebellion. With the final surrender of Galway in May 1652, the entire country was subdued. The final price of the decade of war was high, with famine, abject poverty and disease rampant throughout the country.

After the end of the civil war there was immense pressure on the English government to settle debts, both to the 'adventurers' who had financed the war and to the soldiers who had fought in it; Irish land was to be the principal currency used. A massive programme of confiscations began, aimed at transplanting all Irish landowners to Connacht and Clare, and distributing their land to the government's creditors. In all, 11,000,000 acres of land were seized, to be divided among 1,000 adventurers and 35,000 soldiers. Although in some ways successful, effecting a huge transfer of land ownership in a very short time, the results were not always as intended. The main class affected by transplantation was that of uninfluential landowners; those at the very top of the scale, the great magnates, and those at the bottom, the tenants and landless, remained where they were, while many of the adventurers and soldiers to whom land was given simply sold out as soon as possible; less than a quarter of them eventually settled in Ireland.

Despite the disasters of the first half of the seventeenth century, many of the native Irish still cherished hopes of regaining their ancestral lands, and the restoration of the Stuart kings of England provided a natural focus for these hopes. Faced with the threat of a fast-expanding Protestant population, swelled during the 1650s by the continuing influx of Scots Presbyterians and the arrival of the Quakers, Baptists and Congregationalists, the Catholics enthusiastically welcomed the accession of James II to the English throne in 1685 and embraced his policy of Catholicization with relish; by the end of 1688 Catholics were dominant in the army, the judiciary, the administration and the town corporations. When James lost his throne to his Protestant son-in-law, William of Orange, Ireland was the natural base from which to attempt to regain it.

By the time he arrived in Ireland in March 1689, only Enniskillen and Londonderry remained under Protestant control. Despite a massive siege mounted against it by James, Londonderry managed to hold out, a victory which proved to be of great significance in the campaign. After this, James remained somewhat inactive until William arrived at Carrickfergus in June 1690. The decisive confrontation between the two armies took place at the Boyne in July 1690, where William triumphed. The Jacobite armies retreated west across the country, and James himself fled to France. The war continued for another fifteen months, until October 1691, when it was formally ended by the Treaty of Limerick.

One of the most important provisions of this treaty was to permit Jacobite officers and men to go into exile. More than 11,000 sailed to France, where they joined the French army and formed the famous Irish Brigade. This, the 'Flight of the Wild Geese', was the start of a long tradition of Irish service in the Continental armies, with more than half a million Irishmen joining the French army alone between 1691 and 1791. From these men descend many renowned French families, such as MacMahon, Lally, O'Farrell and O'Kelly.

The end of the Williamite War marked the final success of English rule in Ireland, and began a period in which the new settlers of the seventeenth century could begin to feel themselves secure in their possessions, and at home in their new country. Over the course of the century, a huge transfer in land ownership had been imposed – in 1603, 90 per cent of Irish land had been in the hands of Catholics, while by 1691 they owned less than 14 per cent. In the process a massive influx of English and Scots had taken place which, in the case of Ulster in particular, radically altered the composition of society.

The old Gaelic world was never to recover from the final collapse of the seventeenth century. Although vestiges of the old culture survived underground in poetry, music and folklore, English ways were now dominant, and this extended even to the old surnames. From about this time, the prefixes O and Mac began to be dropped, and the names themselves were anglicised and distorted. English officials and landlords, unfamiliar with Irish, transliterated, translated, and mistranslated. Thus, for example, *Ó hArrachtáin*, common in Cork and Kerry, was changed to Harrington, its nearest-sounding English equivalent. Other names were translated, *Mac Gabhann* (son of the smith) becoming Smith in some areas, while remaining McGowan in others, and *Mac Giolla Easpaig* (son of the follower of the bishop) becoming either Gillespie or, simply, Bishop. A large number of ludicrous mistranslations also date from this time. To take one example only: *Mac an Déaghanaigh* (son of the dean) became Bird in many places, because of a spurious phonetic resemblance to the Irish for bird, *éan*. Previous Gaelic attitudes to such names underline the sharp ironies of this process. When the influx of settlers began in the seventeenth century, the Gaelic poets ridiculed the new surnames; in Irish society, the function of the surname, with O or Mac, was to indicate kinship, and such names as White, Black, Bird or Smith were simply absurd and laughable. Within less than a century, the names they had mocked were being forced on them.

William of Orange, whose victories in Ireland signalled the
end of any hope for the restoration of the old Gaelic order.

Newcomers and Emigrants

Around the start of the eighteenth century, as Irish conditions became more settled, two groups of Continental Protestant refugees were settled in the country with official or semi-official help. The first of these, the Huguenots, were French Calvinists persecuted intermittently by the Catholic rulers of France throughout the seventeenth century. Small numbers of refugees from this persecution had come to Ireland, mainly via England, from 1620 to 1641, and again with Cromwell in 1649, but it was in 1685, after the revocation of the Edict of Nantes, which had guaranteed them toleration, that the main body of Huguenots began to

The Irish House of Commons, though rigidly confined to the Anglo-Irish, became the focus for a growing sense of independence and Irish identity in the eighteenth century.

arrive, mostly from the countryside around the city of La Rochelle in the modern region of Poitou-Charente. After the end of the Williamite wars, large Huguenot settlements were established in Portarlington, Youghal, Cork, Dublin, Waterford and Lisburn, where they became celebrated for their expertise in textiles, specialising in weaving, lace-making, and glove-making. In the course

Jonathan Swift, son of an English immigrant to Ireland, and confidant of English prime ministers, exhorted his Irish readers to "burn everything English but their coal".

of time, they became thoroughly absorbed into Irish society through intermarriage, and names such as Boucicault, Maturin, Le Fanu and Trench are still familiar in Ireland today.

The Palatines

The second wave of Protestant refugees were the Palatine Germans. In early May 1709, thousands of the inhabitants of the countryside of Hesse and Baden, near the city of Mannheim, were forced off their land by the wars between Louis XIV and a confederacy that included England. They made their way to Rotterdam, and from there to London in English ships. The English appear to have been ill-prepared to receive them, and over 800 families, more than 6,000 people, were despatched to Ireland between September 1709 and January 1710.

Initially there was some difficulty in placing the Palatines; of 538 families first taken on as tenants by Anglo-Irish landlords, 352 were reported to have deserted their holdings, and a good number of these returned to England. However, some of the settlements were highly successful, in particular that on the Southwell lands around Rathkeale in Co. Limerick in 1712. One hundred and fifty families settled here on very favourable terms, and within a few years were fully engaged in the production of hemp, flax and cattle. A second successful and sizeable settlement of Palatine families was carried out on the lands of Abel Ram, near Gorey in Co. Wexford around the same period. The distinctive Palatine way of life endured in these areas until well into the nineteenth century. Evidence of their eventual full absorption into the life of the country is found today in the geographical spread of the distinctive surnames of their descendants: Switzer, Ruttle, Sparling, Tesky and Fitzell.

The Anglo-Irish

Along with these readily-identifiable immigrant groups, the eighteenth century also saw the rise of a much more powerful, though less well defined race, the Anglo-Irish. These were a social elite, dominating politics, the law, land, and the professions, who were descended from Norman, Old English, Cromwellian or even, in some rare cases, Old Gaelic stock. Rather than a common ethnic origin, what defined this people was their own sense of belonging, derived from a confused colonial nationalism. This is reflected in their use of the word 'Irish'. Those who, in 1690, were 'the Protestants of Ireland' or 'the English of this Kingdom', by the 1720s could call themselves, simply, 'Irish gentlemen'; whereas previously 'Irish' had meant 'native Irish', it was now extended to cover those who had been outsiders. There remained, however, a fatal ambiguity in its use. The continuing threat posed to the position of the Anglo-Irish by the overwhelming majority of the population – Gaelic, Catholic, and living in a degree of poverty that astounded foreign observers – meant that they simply could not afford to identify too closely with the country as a whole. As a result, in the writings of the time 'the Irish', or even 'the Irish race' most often refers specifically to the people we now call Anglo-Irish.

The best-known representative of the Anglo-Irish was Dr Jonathan Swift, poet, satirist, and Dean of St Patrick's Cathedral, Dublin, and the dilemma of his race is illustrated vividly in his work. Fighting bitterly against the poverty and injustice which he saw inflicted on

The design for the funeral of the Countess of Ormond in 1601, as recorded by a contemporary heraldic artist. The love of elaborate ceremonial was always a feature of the Anglo-Irish Establishment.

Ireland by the self-interest of the English government, his struggle was nonetheless largely on behalf of his fellow Irish Protestants. At the same time, he was aware that such formulations of his as 'government without the consent of the governed is the very definition of slavery' could apply just as well to the relationship between Anglo-Irish and Gaelic Irish as it could to the relationship between the English government and the Anglo-Irish. In attacking injustice done to his own race, he was in the peculiar and uncomfortable position of implicitly attacking injustice done by them. In Swift's case at least, common humanity could outweigh partisan considerations, and some of his most famous work is universal in its implications. *A Modest Proposal*, for instance, in response to mass starvation among the most destitute Irish, satirically suggests selling their young children as food for gentlemen, even offering some helpful recipes.

Although real power emanated from London, within Ireland the Anglo-Irish were dominant for over two centuries, and much of the character of the country today derives from their influence. They were responsible for the great neo-classical houses of the gentry, the Georgian buildings and thoroughfares of Dublin, and the literary tradition which lay behind the great revival of writing in Ireland in the early twentieth century.

The Penal Laws

In homogenizing the mixed origins of the Anglo-Irish, the one decisive factor was Anglicanism; membership of the Church of Ireland was an absolute prerequisite for advancement or power. The key mechanism for the retention and reinforcement of this power was provided by a whole series of measures, known collectively as the Penal Laws. In theory, these placed fanatically detailed restrictions on the property rights, social rights and religious practice of non-Anglicans, denying them, for example, the right to take leases or own land above a certain value, outlawing Catholic clergy, forbidding higher education and entry to the professions, and imposing oaths of conformity to the state church, the Church of Ireland. Thorough enforcement of many of these laws was never a practical proposition, given the make-up of the population, but they nonetheless had a profound effect. To take one area only, by the time the laws began to be relaxed somewhat in the 1770s, only five per cent of the land of the country remained in Catholic hands.

Ulster Emigration

Although more than a quarter of the population of Ireland in the eighteenth century was Protestant, the Anglo-Irish Anglicans made up only a minority of this. It was the Ulster settlers and their descendants, overwhelmingly Presbyterian, who were in the the majority. The Penal Laws, designed as they were to protect the privileges of members of the Church of Ireland, disenfranchised and discriminated against Presbyterians as well as Catholics, though the effects were mitigated to some extent by their superior economic strength and the tight-knit communities in which they lived. Nonetheless, to a people who had originally fled Scotland to escape religious persecution, the impositions of the Penal Laws were intolerable. This was reflected in the increasing radicalization of Ulster opinion, which was to reach its peak in the rebellion of 1798, but also in emigration from Ulster to America. This was the start of a process with far-reaching consequences. Up to now, the movement of peoples had been into Ireland. Now began the long exodus.

As well as political discontent, this first movement of emigration also had economic causes. The large majority of Ulster Presbyterians were poor smallholders,

artisans, weavers and labourers, all most vulnerable both to the succession of natural disasters – crop failures, smallpox epidemics, livestock diseases – which recurred throughout the eighteenth century, and to the increasing commercialization of Ulster, with the constant efforts of landlords to increase the profitability of their lands by raising rents. The increasing importance of the linen trade was also influential, and the numbers of emigrants grew and fell as this trade prospered or faltered. The very nature of the business facilitated emigration, since the ships which brought flax seed from America often returned with a cargo of emigrants. Before 1720 the stream of migrants across the Atlantic was slow but steady, with New England the favoured

Above: the wild splendour of the Wicklow Mountains framed by the elegant terracing of Powerscourt Demesne. For the Anglo-Irish, part of the charm of such careful landscaping would have come from its reflection of the political relationship between themselves and the Gaelic Irish. Trinity College, Dublin (left) was at the very heart of the Anglo-Irish Establishment.

destination. After that date, the rate of emigration grew, with a peak in the late 1720s, and a decline in the 1730s, when relative prosperity returned to Ulster. The famine of 1740-41 gave a sharp impetus to the renewal of emigration, which rose steadily through the 1760s, when over 20,000 people left from the Ulster ports of Newry,

Portrush, Belfast, Larne and Londonderry. The migration reached a climax in the years 1770-74, when at least 30,000 people departed. Over the course of the whole century, it is estimated that more than 400,000 emigrated from Ulster, the vast majority to North America; in 1790, the United States' population of Irish stock has been estimated at 447,000, two-thirds of them originating from Ulster.

Those who left were mostly indentured labourers, contracting to work for a number of years for employers in Colonial America in return for their passage, and included very few convicts or independent travellers. One important result, and a significant difference with later, Catholic, emigration, is the fact that the move was often effected by entire families or even communities, allowing the settlers to maintain their way of life in the New World, and providing a continuity of religion and

Charles Carroll (above left), whose grandfather left Ireland for America in 1688, was the only Catholic signatory of the Declaration of Independence. Presidents Andrew Jackson (top) and Woodrow Wilson (above) are among the most prominent of the descendants of the eighteenth-century Scots-Irish emigrants.

tradition in keeping with the religious and cultural separateness they had already brought with them from Scotland to Ireland. To point up this separateness, in America they called themselves 'Scots-Irish', and the distinctive culture they maintained allows us to trace their settlements in the United States with some precision. Initially, most of the emigrants sailed to the Delaware estuary, especially to Pennsylvania, where Cumberland County became the effective centre of the

Scots-Irish settlement. In the 1730s, a second wave of emigrants, accompanied by the children of earlier settlers, moved further west in Pennsylvania and south into the Valley of Virginia. By the 1750s a third movement pushed further south again into the Carolina and Georgia back-country, where they met and mixed with emigrants arriving through southern seaports such as Charleston and Savannah. By the 1790s more than half the settlers along the Appalachian frontier were of Ulster lineage. The influence of their culture, their music, religion and way of life, can still be seen in these areas today.

The blend of Protestant evangelism, fierce self-sufficiency and political radicalism which many Ulster Presbyterians brought with them to the New World was powerfully influential in the American Revolution. In all the states, but especially in Pennsylvania, New Jersey, New York, Delaware and Maryland, the immigrant Scots-Irish and their descendants played a role in the war out of all proportion to their numbers; as an officer on the British side put it, 'call this war by whatever name you may, only call it not an American rebellion; it is nothing more or less than a Scotch Irish Presbyterian rebellion'. After American independence, the Scots-Irish tradition continued to play an important part in American life; the great nineteenth-century steel-producing town of Pittsburgh was created by Scots-Irish entrepreneurs, and their representatives are found at all levels of American society, in the professions, industry, finance, education, and with presidents such as Andrew Jackson and Woodrow Wilson.

1798

Ulster radicalism also found another outlet at home. Throughout the eighteenth century, local secret societies, such as the 'Hearts of Steel' and the 'Hearts of Oak', had sprung up, dedicated to defending their members, generally the poorest tenants. This tradition, along with the influence of the French and American Revolutions, provided the background for the United Irishmen, an organization dedicated to republican ideals and incorporating Catholic, Presbyterian and Anglo-Irish radicals. On May 23rd 1798, a rebellion against British rule organized by the United Irishmen broke out, with risings in Meath, Carlow, Kildare, Wicklow, Dublin and Wexford in the east, Antrim and Down in Ulster, and, with the assistance of a French invasion, in Mayo in the west. Over the course of the next six months the

Mathew Carey was forced to flee Ireland in 1784 for criticising the British government in print. He continued his radical journalism in the United States.

rebellion was crushed by the British, at great cost to lives and property; over 30,000 people died, and a million pounds worth of property was destroyed. Although the ideals of fraternity and religious equality which inspired the United Irishmen were defeated, many of the post-1798 refugees to the United States took those ideals with them, and many of them rose to social and political prominence. Another result of the failure of 1798 was an increase in pressure for Union between Ireland and Britain. The subsequent abolition of the Irish parliament and Irish self-government was one of the reasons for the huge increase in emigration from Ireland in the nineteenth century.

For the vast majority of those who emigrated, the Atlantic represented
an insuperable obstacle to return, as final as death itself.

Emigration and the Famine

The traditional view of emigration in Presbyterian Ulster differed greatly from the image prevalent among the great mass of the population: the Gaelic Catholics. Whereas, in the popular mythology of the Scots-Irish, the New World offered an almost biblical deliverance from religious intolerance and economic oppression, for the Catholics emigration meant exile, in the phrase used by the Irish monastic missionaries of the early middle ages, a 'white martyrdom', second in suffering only to death itself. Allied to this overwhelmingly negative view of emigration, related, no doubt, to the traditional importance of extended kin-relationships in

The rock-strewn landscape of the Curraghmore Valley, Co. Kerry.

Gaelic life and strengthened by the enforced departure of the Gaelic aristocracy in the seventeenth century, were the practical barriers. Until 1780, Catholic immigration was officially forbidden in the Americas, and even if they possessed the inclination and the ingenuity to get to America, few of the Catholic Irish had the means. Nonetheless, some Catholic emigration did take place. As a result of the trade between the American

Victorian workhouses in Ireland were deliberately harsh and inhumane, to prevent 'abuse' by the lazy. By the middle of the nineteenth century mass desperation had swamped the system.

colonies and such southern ports as Cork and Kinsale, some Catholic Irish did manage to settle in the new colonies, particularly in Virginia and Maryland, where such names as 'New Ireland' and 'New Munster' appear. The most substantial Irish connection at this period, however, was with the West Indies. In the seventeenth century, in the aftermath of the Cromwellian wars, substantial numbers of the most destitute were shipped as slaves to 'the Barbadoes', and relatively large numbers of voluntary emigrants are also recorded in Jamaica, the Leeward Islands, and Montserrat, as well as in Barbados. As the slave-based economy of these areas grew, however, opportunities for poor white settlers diminished, and during the 1700s most of the Irish Catholics moved from the West Indies to the mainland

colonies. Another route for emigrants at this period was to Newfoundland, which maintained strong ties with Waterford and Wexford. In 1776, three to five thousand were reported to be leaving annually from these areas on Newfoundland ships, and by 1784 seven-eighths of the population of St John's, Newfoundland, was Irish-born.

When compared with the exodus from Ulster, however, Catholic emigration before the nineteenth century was relatively insignificant. Even after 1780, when the new egalitarian republic of the United States might have been expected to attract large numbers, migration remained very low. In part, this was due to new practical problems: the series of wars lasting right up to the final defeat of Napoleon in 1814 severely disrupted shipping, and made the journey across the Atlantic dangerous and difficult. There is no doubt, though, that relative prosperity at home, combined with the continuing view of emigration as a last resort, were the principal brakes on potential emigration.

Australia

The negative popular vision of emigration can only have been reinforced by the start of transportation of Irish convicts to Australia in 1780. The offences for which transportation could be imposed were manifold, ranging from the pettiest of thefts to 'treasonous' political crimes; by 1803, of the 2,086 Irish convicts in Australia, 40 per cent were political prisoners and the remainder sentenced for criminal offences. By 1836 there were about 20,000 Irish in the country and in 1861, three years after transportation had ended, the Irish community constituted almost 20 per cent of the population of Australia. Because of the distance involved, the journey was very costly, and this meant that very few arrived without assistance of some sort, either the unwelcome assistance of transportation, or one of the many schemes, in general privately funded, which evolved over the course of the nineteenth century. These schemes to subsidize the cost of the journey were aimed specifically at encouraging the migration of family groups and those with skills, and resulted in many communities leaving en masse; once a network of family ties existed in Australia into which new emigrants could fit, the breaking of the links with Ireland became easier. In the late nineteenth century, during the New Zealand gold rush, the numbers of Irish entering that country grew dramatically, and a strong Irish settlement developed along the west coast. Although the smaller population of New Zealand meant there were fewer obstacles to intermarriage and social mobility, Irish Catholics still faced many of the same disadvantages as they did in Australia and, to some extent, America: anti-Catholic prejudice, resentment against rural immigrants living in urban conditions, discrimination in housing and employment. As in America, these were ultimately overcome in Australia and New Zealand through growing power in the labour associations, the political parties, and the Church itself. Even at its height, however, it must be said that emigrants to Australia and New Zealand remained only a small fraction of the total numbers leaving the country in the nineteenth century.

Pre-Famine Emigration

The great flood of emigration which was permanently to alter the character of Ireland began in the early decades of the nineteenth century. Although many other factors contributed to it, the most fundamental underlying cause was population growth. At the start of the eighteenth century, the most reliable estimates put the total population of the country at around two million. By 1754 this had risen to only 2.3 million, a tiny rate of growth by contemporary standards, due to poverty, disease and Ulster emigration. By 1800, the number was between 4,500,000 and 5,000,000, in the 1821 census it was recorded as 6,800,000, and by 1841 it was 8,200,000. This increase was largely concentrated in the period from about 1780 to 1830, and overwhelmingly affected the poorest, labouring classes. What caused such rapid growth is still a matter of controversy, but some of the possible reasons are clear: traditionally, marriage ages in Ireland were relatively young, leading to very large families, and the subdivision of holdings enforced by the Penal Laws permitted increasing numbers to marry and stay on the land, albeit at the cost of a continually poorer standard of living. It seems clear as well that the relative prosperity brought about by rising prices during the period of the Napoleonic wars, from 1790 to 1814, encouraged early marriage, lowered infant mortality and made it possible for more people to exist off smaller holdings. At any rate, the stark fact is that over seventy or so years the population of the country almost quadrupled; since the vast majority were already living in the most abject poverty even before this increase, a disaster was clearly in the making.

In the aftermath of the Napoleonic wars, from 1814, came an immediate and dramatic economic slump: prices fell catastrophically, major industries collapsed, investment and growth stagnated, and unemployment and destitution became widespread. The depression lasted for almost two decades, and was accompanied by a series of natural catastrophes. In 1816-18, bad weather destroyed grain and potato crops, and smallpox and typhus killed over 50,000 people. The potato crop failed again in Munster in 1821, and people starved to death in Cork and Clare. After further crop failures in 1825-30, famine was only averted by the import of large amounts of Indian meal from America, and in 1832 'stark famine' struck Munster and south Leinster. Throughout the early 1830s cholera repeatedly ravaged the poorest classes and, in the decade as a whole, the potato crop failed on a local level in eight out of the ten years. There was a savage winter in 1838, and 'the night

of the big wind', in which snow buried the cottages and cattle froze to death in the fields. Finally, in 1840-44, the potato crops partly failed three more times. Small wonder that the Irish should feel God had abandoned them. 'There is a Distruction Approaching to Ireland', wrote one emigrant, 'their time is nerely at an end'.

From 1814, the shipping lanes to North America, which had been closed by the war, were reopened, and mass emigration restarted. In 1815-16 alone, over 20,000 crossed from Ireland to North America. At first, the pattern was very similar to the earlier migrations; about two-thirds of those leaving in the years 1815-19 were from Ulster, and many were people in the class above the very poorest – artisans, shopkeepers, 'strong' farmers and professionals – more often than not travelling in family groups. This was largely because British legislation discriminated against United States shipping, and thus kept the cost of passage prohibitively high. For the same reason, most of these emigrants went to British North America, rather than to the U.S.A., travelling in returning Canadian timber ships. The vast majority pushed on from Canada to the United States, where there were family or community links, although increasing numbers now began to stay in the rapidly expanding colony, often encouraged by government grants of land.

Over the course of the next two decades, as economic depression and natural disasters took their toll, the character of the emigration began to change. Despite the continuing high fares, more and more of those leaving were from the labouring classes, the poorest, who somehow managed prices for the passage ranging from £4 to £10 per person. Similarly, the religious make-up of those leaving was altering. More and more Catholics were now leaving, some assisted by such schemes as that briefly implemented by the British government in 1823-25, which provided free passage and land grants to over 2,500 Catholic smallholders, primarily from the Mallow and Fermoy districts of north Cork. The biggest single spur to such emigration, however, came in 1827, when the government repealed all restrictions on emigration; between 1828 and 1837 almost 400,000 Irish people left for North America. Up to 1832, about half of the emigrants still came from Ulster, but after that date the three southern provinces contributed the majority, and from now on, although a steady stream of Northern Protestants continued to

emigrate, encouraged by the established Scots-Irish community, their proportion of total emigration was in continuous decline.

Up to the 1830s, the favoured route for the emigrants was still to Canada, and from there to the United States. The majority of departures were from Irish ports, with Belfast, Londonderry and Dublin now the most important. However, over the 1830s, as trade increased between Liverpool and the U.S., the cost of the the direct journey dropped, and increasing numbers crossed to Liverpool and from there made their way to New York, Boston and Philadelphia. For the very poorest Britain became the final destination; those who could not afford even the lower fares across the Atlantic paid the few pence for deck passage across the Irish sea. Conditions on such crossings were appalling. Deck passengers had a lower priority than baggage or livestock, and up to 2,000 people could be crowded onto an open deck in all weathers, clinging to each other to avoid being washed overboard. In 1830-35 200,000 Irish people made such crossings, and by 1841 over 400,000 lived permanently in Britain, mostly in the largest cities: Glasgow, London, Manchester, and Liverpool itself.

Between 1838 and 1844, the patterns were set which would make possible the massive Famine and post-Famine departures; large numbers of southern Catholic Irish left from all areas of the country, establishing both an example for the future and a community of sorts which could absorb new arrivals, and the Liverpool-New York route had become routine and relatively cheap. Although Ulster emigration continued, more emigrants now took ship at Cork than at Belfast, and large numbers also left from such ports as Limerick and Sligo. Many of those disembarking at Canadian and American ports are described as desperately poor, but in fact, even at this stage, the majority of those leaving did not come from the very poorest classes. Even in the 1840s officials and landlords continued to complain that those who were going were the 'better sort'. As one Protestant clergyman put it, 'the young, the enterprising and the industrious leave us, while the old, the idle and indolent portions, the dregs, stay with us.'

The old attitudes to emigration changed slowly in the years leading up to the Famine. At first, the old, negative view persisted. In the years after the end of the

The pressure of world opinion did more to prompt British action than the needs of those who were starving. Help from the United States was practical as well as political; huge amounts of money were sent by earlier emigrants to help the departure of those still remaining.

Napoleonic wars, according to a Dublin newspaper, 'the native Irish' still held 'a vehement and, in many instances, an absurd attachment to the soil on which they were born.' This traditional hostility to emigration was strongest in those areas of the country where the old Gaelic traditions survived, on the western coasts and in other remote, mountainous regions, densely populated and suffering the greatest poverty. For these people, emigration was still banishment, still the greatest evil next to death. Even here, however, as the deprivations of the 1820s and 1830s deepened, some emigration occurred, although the great exodus from these areas did not come until the 1880s. In other, more anglicized districts of the country, emigrants' letters often painted an unrealistically bright picture of the life which awaited their friends and relatives across the Atlantic and, as more and more people left, the prospect of uprooting

and moving became less unknown and threatening. Even for those who thought of emigration as escape from economic and social oppression, however, there were severe cultural, social and even psychological problems; the rupture with the still powerfully influential traditions of extended community and family remained extremely painful for all who left.

The Famine

For the great mass of the people of Ireland, subsistence was made possible by one thing alone, the potato. Described by modern nutritionists as the one staple food capable of sustaining life as a sole diet, it had been common in Ireland since the seventeenth century, and was already at that point identified with Ireland in the eyes of some foreigners: anti-Irish mobs in seventeenth-century England are described as having used a potato impaled on a stick to represent the Irish. At that time, however, and during the early part of the eighteenth century, it formed only the basic part of a diet which also included milk, buttermilk, eggs, fish, and meat for the better-off. As the pressures of population grew through the last part of the eighteenth century and into the nineteenth century, for large numbers of people it went from being an important food to being the only food. Since a single acre of potatoes could feed a family of six, it was the basis of survival of the very poorest. Contemporary accounts describe the Irish eating huge quantities, an average, according to contemporary statistics, of ten pounds a day per person.

Partial failures of the potato crop, and resulting local famines, were relatively common up to the 1840s. In 1845, however, a previously unknown blight appeared without warning and destroyed the potatoes so rapidly that terror was spread throughout the countryside. 'The air was laden with a sickly odour of decay, as if the hand of death had stricken the potato field, and everything growing in it was rotten.' That year, only 30 to 40 per cent of the crop was actually destroyed, and though there was great suffering, few starved; people ate food normally sold to pay rent, pawned clothes, depended on public relief. All of these could only be temporary measures, and everything depended on the following year's crop. In late July and early August 1846 the blight returned, and this time, with astonishing rapidity, destroyed almost the entire potato crop. Less than one fifth of the harvest survived. In 1847, although the blight eased because so few potatoes were sown, the harvest was only ten per cent of the 1844 level. Encouraged by the relative healthiness of the 1847 crop, mass planting took place once more, but the blight returned in full force in 1848, with the countryside 'from sea to sea one mass of unvaried rottenness and decay'. Blight continued to ravage the crop for the following six years, and it was not until 1855 that the total harvest reached more than half of what it had been in 1844.

From the summer of 1846 on, the blight brought immediate and horrible distress. One historian estimates that between 1.1 and 1.5 million people died of starvation and famine-related diseases, and scenes of unimaginable mass suffering were witnessed: 'cowering wretches almost naked in the savage weather, prowling in turnip fields and endeavouring to grub up roots', 'famished and ghastly skeletons, such as no words can describe', 'little children, their limbs fleshless, their faces bloated, yet wrinkled and of a pale greenish hue'. Deaths were highest in south Ulster, west Munster and Connacht, those parts of the country where the population of poorest subsistence farmers and labourers was most dense, but very few areas escaped entirely; all over the country landless labourers died in their tens of thousands, and even shopkeepers, townspeople, and relatively comfortable farmers perished from the effects of the diseases spread by the starving and destitute.

Although the blight itself was unavoidable, its impact on Ireland was magnified by the response of the British government. Blinkered by free-market dogma, and by a profound, almost malevolent indifference to Irish ills, the government refused to recognize the scale of the disaster or to provide public assistance above the level existing before 1844. Only after the horrors of the winter of 1847, when world opinion made it impossible to ignore the magnitude of the cataclysm occurring in Ireland, were efforts finally made to organize public relief. Even then, these efforts were hampered by slavish adherence to the ideals of the free-marketeers: the poor could not be allowed to become dependent on the state and, above all, the market itself should not be interfered with. As a result, thousands of starving people were put to work, for barely enough to keep them alive from day to day, on projects with no practical value, such as unnecessary bridges, and roads that led from nowhere to nowhere.

Famine Emigration

The effect of the Great Famine on emigration was immediate and dramatic. Between 1845 and 1855, almost 1.5 million people embarked for the United States; 340,000 sailed for British North America; around 300,000 settled in the cities of Great Britain, and about 70,000 went to Australia. In all, more than 2.1 million people left Ireland in these eleven years, over a quarter of the pre-Famine population, and greater than the combined total of all those who had left in the previous two-and-a-half centuries. Together with the huge Famine death-rate among children, the result was the disappearance of almost an entire generation: less than one in three of those born in the early 1830s died in Ireland of old age.

To some extent the enormous wave of Famine emigration followed earlier patterns. Those districts which were poor but not utterly destitute – east Connacht, south Ulster and the Leinster midlands – contributed the greatest numbers. Areas like west Cork and south Londonderry, densely populated by the poorest subsistence farmers, suffered appalling death rates, while east Cork and north Londonderry, relatively more prosperous, lost huge numbers through emigration. Only north Connacht experienced simultaneously high rates of death and emigration. Nevertheless, there were significant differences from earlier migrations. Whereas only 60 per cent of those arriving at New York were classed as 'labourers' in 1836, by 1851-55 the proportion had risen to between 79 and 90 per cent. More than ever before, these people needed financial assistance to pay for the crossing, and this generally came from relatives. A family would combine their money, or borrow, to send one son or cousin to the U.S., he would then send back money to bring out another member of the family, and in this way, little by little, entire families, or even communities, would manage to get away. A huge amount of money poured into Ireland from America, particularly in the early 1850s, to be used to finance the departure of further emigrants.

A change also came about in the prevailing attitudes to emigration. Where previously there had been at least some measure of choice in the decision to leave, and pain at the breaking of communal ties, the dominant note now was desperation, panic even. Most earlier emigrants had been sensitive to reports of hard times in

Emigrants leaving Queenstown (now Cobh) for New York in 1874. The introduction of steamships on the Atlantic route dramatically reduced the length, and the horrors, of the journey.

the U.S. and difficulties in the journey; now the exodus continued to grow even in the face of the most discouraging reports from abroad and the savage hardships of a mid-winter Atlantic crossing. As one group pleaded, 'all we want is to get out of Ireland, we must be better anywhere than here'. Despair was the driving force in a panic-stricken scramble for survival.

Desperation was also reflected in the changing routes for emigration. Previously, passengers had embarked at the major ports in Ireland, or from Liverpool. Now emigrant ships left from small, little-used ports such as Westport, Kinsale and Killala. Some idea of the conditions endured by the people on board such ships can be gleaned from the story of one, the *Elizabeth and Sarah*, which left Killala in May 1847. The vessel, built in

1763, was 83 years old, and carried 276 passengers, 121 more than the legal limit. For all these people there were only 36 berths. During the voyage, no food was given to the passengers, who had to rely on whatever they had managed to bring on board, and a maximum of only two pints of water per person per day was allocated. When she arrived off Quebec, after a journey of 41 days, all the water on board was unfit to drink, 18 people, including the master of the ship, had died of fever and the remainder were starving. In some respects, considering the condition of the ship, those who survived were lucky: on some of the 'coffin ships' the death rates were 30 per cent and more. For those attempting to use the Liverpool route, as well as overcrowding, starvation and disease, the dangers included unscrupulous middlemen and landlords, thieves, conmen, and the extortionate tactics of ships' agents and owners. Still, with the only alternative a slow death at home, hundreds of thousands faced and overcame these horrifying obstacles.

Young Irish-Americans watching the St Patrick's Day parade,
still a display of pride in both homelands, old and new.

Irish America and the Effects of Emigration

The experience of the Famine emigrants in America was also different from that of their predecessors. The sheer scale of the influx flooded the labour market, leaving the vast majority of the newcomers clustered together in poverty in ghettoes in the cities of the east coast: New York, Philadelphia and Boston. In New York City in 1850, 30,000 people, most of them Irish, were living below ground level in cellars often flooded by rainwater or sewage. Such work as there was, for example on the construction of the Erie canal and the railroads, tended to be harsh and poorly paid, and traditional animosity towards Irish Catholics resulted in institutional

A pipe band plays before a hurling match. The late ninteenth-century revival of sport and culture was only possible with Irish-American support.

discrimination and injustice: mob violence, underpaid (or unpaid) wages, 'No Irish Need Apply' notices, these were the common experience for the decades up to the 1870s. Significant numbers of those who emigrated simply failed to survive; one Irish-American wrote that 'the average life of an emigrant after landing here is six years, and many insist it is much less'. Certainly, it was only after 1870 that Irish-American society began to

coalesce and stabilize, finding protection and strength through the institutions of the Catholic Church and the Democratic Party, and even then a large minority of Irish-Americans remained amongst the poorest and most deprived.

From the 1870s on, Irish-America had a voice, not only in the United States itself, but also in the politics of Ireland. Large numbers of Irish-Americans simply blamed Britain for having forced them to emigrate, seeing their departure as a direct result of political oppression, rather than economic necessity, and the very real British mismanagement and indifference during the Famine left a legacy of intense bitterness which found expression in fervent support for the successive nationalist movements of the late nineteenth and early twentieth centuries. Such Irish-American societies as Clan na Gael in the 1870s, the National League of

America in the 1880s, and de Valera's American Association for the Recognition of the Irish Republic in 1919-21 played a vital role in providing support for the Land League, the Fenians, the Home Rule movement and Sinn Féin in Ireland itself. It is doubtful if any of the changes brought about by these movements, including the ultimate independence of the 26 southern counties in 1921, could have been achieved without the moral and financial backing of Irish-America. Such backing continues right up to the present.

In America itself, the Irish played a part that was almost equally important. The close community ties which the emigrants brought with them provided the basis for a tightly organized political machine which, through the Democratic Party, achieved local power and then increasing national influence until, by 1963, the President, the Speaker of the House of

Representatives, the Majority Leader of the Senate, and the Chairman of the National Committee were all Irish-American Catholic Democrats. With political power came relative wealth and increasing assimilation. As growing prosperity allowed the Irish to move out of ghetto areas the old ties weakened, but the general characteristics of their culture remained: hardworking and materialist, socially conservative, family-centred, and with a great residue of nostalgia for Ireland itself.

Post-Famine Emigration

In the history of other nations, such catastrophes as the Famine have slowed the growth of the population only temporarily. In Ireland's case, however, the great explosion of emigration during the Famine years simply accelerated a trend already present; the total population declined from around 8.5 million in 1845 to 5.8 million in 1861, and continued to shrink, to less than 4.3 million in 1926. In the 80 years before 1926, the country lost an estimated 4.1 million inhabitants to emigration. Somewhere between half a million and a million went to Great Britain, to the South Wales coalfields and the great industrial metropolises of Scotland and England. Many of these eventually joined the vast majority, over three million, who went directly to the United States, so that the total for American emigration probably reaches more than three-and-a-half million for these years. Of the rest, around 200,000 went to Canada, almost 300,000 to Australia and New Zealand, and another 60,000 or so to Argentina, South Africa and other destinations. The U.S., though, was the overwhelming choice of the emigrants; by 1900 it contained more Irish than Ireland itself.

The reasons for the continued vast migration are, on the face of it, varied. The American Civil War produced a large demand for manpower in the early 1860s, particularly in the industries and army of the North; over 200,000 Irishmen fought in the war, the overwhelming majority for the North, and many of these were recruited in Ireland by agents who offered free passage and substantial bounties (by Irish standards). The journey itself began to hold fewer terrors, as steamships cut the travelling time, competition reduced fares and government regulation improved conditions on board. In America, the growing power of the Irish-American community afforded some welcome protection from the uncertainties of starting a

new life. In Ireland there was an increasing determination not to subdivide further small family farms, which meant that only one son could expect to stay. But the single most important factor in sustaining the flood of emigration was economic deprivation. Mass evictions, the near-famines of 1861-64 and 1879-82, the continual

Facing page: the Gaelic Society's hurling and football team, which played throughout the northeastern U.S. in 1890-2. Above: Sunday morning Mass for Irish-American soldiers of the Union in Arlington, Virginia, in 1861.

grinding poverty of subsistence farming; these ensured that for the vast majority any opportunity to improve their lives would be gladly welcomed, and the improved ease of emigration simply made it possible for many to take that opportunity.

Emigration in these years also affected areas which had previously remained relatively immune. The most traditional areas of the country, still Irish-speaking, had suffered terrible death-rates in the Famine and its aftermath, but maintained the old resistance to the idea of emigration. The crisis of 1879-82 had a decisive impact on these areas, and that resistance collapsed: a flood of departures began from Kerry, west Cork, west Galway, Mayo and Donegal. 'The full conviction had come upon them,' wrote one observer 'that it was impossible to struggle longer with the depth of poverty by which they had been surrounded.' Between 1881 and

1901 the number of Irish-speakers in Munster and Connacht fell by a third.

The flood to the U.S. continued until the First World War, when shipping was severely disrupted, then resumed, reaching a peak in the years from 1921 to 1923, and finally began to decline. After this, North America ceased to be the most important destination; international depression, American restrictions on immigrants, and the simple fact of population depletion limited the numbers of those departing, and a growing British demand for labour up to the 1960s, together with

As their prosperity and influence grew, the Irish in America retained a strong sense of community, as shown in these pictures taken at the turn of the century in Refugio Co., Texas. Right: Oscar Fagan outside his farmhouse. Below: the Irish gather after Mass.

Throughout the late nineteenth and early twentieth centuries emigration continued to weaken rural communities, and in some cases ultimately destroyed them. The Blasket Islands, Co. Kerry (above) were abandoned by their last inhabitants only in 1953.

the relative ease of transport back and forth between the two islands, meant that Britain now received by far the greatest number of emigrants. The population of the 26 counties of the Republic, around three million in 1921, continued to shrink, to 2.8 million in 1961. It is only in the last two decades that this trend has been reversed, with the current population around 3.5 million. Although it had been hoped that the necessity for emigration had been banished, the last years of the 1980s saw a growth again in the departures of the young to the U.S. and Britain. It seems likely, however, that this is only a temporary phenomenon.

For Northern Ireland the picture is slightly different. Since the creation of the state in 1921, the population has grown from around 1.3 to 1.5 million. This increase reflects the relatively greater prosperity of the area, due to earlier industrialization and better integration into the economy of Great Britain. The increase would be larger were it not for continuing emigration. In the early years of the state, this consisted mostly of Catholics leaving for the U.S., many of them embittered by the outcome of the struggle with the British, the creation of Northern Ireland itself. On the Protestant side, emigration was, and continues to be, almost exclusively to the former British dominions of Canada and Australia; from the end of the nineteenth century these have been favoured over the U.S., principally because of the existence in these places of the strong family and community links provided by such institutions as the Orange Order, but also because the size and power of the Catholic Irish-American influence in the U.S. made it less attractive. With the restrictions placed on immigration by Australia, New Zealand and Canada from the 1960s, this emigration too has now slowed to a trickle.

The Effects of Emigration

The vast exodus of people from Ireland through the nineteenth and into the twentieth century changed the character of the country permanently. This is apparent even on a purely physical level in the appearance of much of Ireland today: the magnificent emptiness of the bogs and mountains of the west, the crumbling, deserted villages, the unspoilt countryside – these are all a direct result of the enforced departure of so many. From being one of the European countries with the highest density of population in the early nineteenth century, Ireland has now become the most thinly populated, with an average number of people per square mile only one tenth that of England. And, since most of the population is now concentrated in the cities of the east coast, this average actually underestimates the emptiness of the rest of the country.

The profound demoralization caused by the Famine and its aftermath produced a widespread feeling that the country was finished, that it could not survive, and this in turn had a dramatic effect on the old, Gaelic culture. To take one aspect only, the Irish language was spoken by around two million people in 1851; by 1971, the official figure was 70,000. The old language was associated with poverty, deprivation and despair; it became identified with failure, of which emigration was overwhelmingly visible proof. Despite heroic efforts to save and revive the language it has now almost disappeared as a living tongue, and at a rate unparalleled in recent European history.

Perhaps the clearest positive effect of emigration, and the resulting creation of large Irish communities overseas, has been an early and sophisticated awareness in Ireland of the country's position in the world. The unique situation of being the first part of the British Empire to become independent, as well as being the only western European country to have been a victim, rather than a practitioner, of imperialism, has given Ireland a role in world affairs out of all proportion to her size, a role supported and made possible by the continuing connections with the overseas Irish.

These pages: the effects of emigration are evident in the Irish countryside even today, in the poignantly unspoilt beauty and the abandoned, decaying cottages.

Above and facing page: the hand-made Book of the
Boyles, showing the descent of the Anglo-Irish Earls of
Cork and Orrery, is a masterpiece of heraldic art.

Acknowledgements

The author and publishers would like to thank all the individuals and organisations who provided advice and assistance throughout the preparation of this book. Special thanks are due to Donal Begley, Chief Herald of Ireland, the Genealogical Office, and to the Genealogical Museum, Dublin, for granting permission to photograph items from their collection.

Picture Credits

The Bettmann Archive: 50 (left); **Bord Failte/Irish Tourist Board**: 14 (bottom), 23 (top and left); **The British Library**: 37; **Michael Diggin Photography**: 8, 11, 14 (top), 17, 18, 25, 31, 52, 65, 66; **Mary Evans Picture Library**: 40, 41, 46; **The Institute of Texan Cultures, San Antonio, Texas**: 64; **Stella Johnson**: 60; **Lotherton Hall (Leeds City Art Gallery)**: 45; **The Library Company of Philadelphia**: 51; **Library of Congress, Washington, D.C.**: 62, 63; **The Mansell Collection**: 54; **The National Gallery of Ireland**: 34 (top); **The New York Historical Society**: 59; **Picturepoint, London**: 20, 24 (bottom), 44; **Tony Ruta, New York**: 33; **Don Sutton International Photo Library**: 15, 19, 34 (bottom), 48-49.
All other photographs Neil Sutherland/Quadrillion Publishing Ltd.
Heraldic device artwork by Myra Maguire